Illus

At Home
Among the
Squirrels

———

NANCY LUSE

———

Grateful acknowledgement is made
to book designer Annie Ellis.

ISBN 978-163684481-7

Printed in the U.S.A by IngramSpark Publishers

This book is first dedicated
to *my mother*, who created fond
memories by reading to me, and
my father, who was a role model
with the way he subscribed to
several newspapers. They fostered
a passion for the written word
in me and my siblings, who
in turn passed it to their children
so that now we have the fourth
generation, joyfully carrying on
the love of books and reading,
as well as writing their own stories.

Using both hands, Jeshu pushed open the trap door above his head and scrambled into the large room of the tree house. The hinges squeaked as he flipped the door onto the floor with a large bang and he reminded himself to bring a can of oil the next time so he could silence the hinges.

"Are you guys coming?" Jeshu asked as his cousin Beniah climbed in behind him.

Following Beniah were his brothers, Elijah and Isaac and bringing up the rear were Jeshu's little brother, Josias, and their sister, Janasa who made sure she was last on the ladder so Josias had someone behind him and wouldn't be afraid.

As for her own state of mind, Janasa wasn't exactly scared, but nevertheless heaved a sigh of relief once she climbed inside the tree house. She looked down, seeing through the branches that the ground was indeed a long way off.

Elijah stood in the middle of the room and checked it out, impressed by the job that Jeshu and Beniah had done with the stack of old boards and large coffee can of nails that their grandfather had given them, along with two saws and a hammer meant for sharing. The two older boys had cut out windows and made a wooden roof that they covered with a plastic tarp as double protection from any rain.

"When do I get to help?" Elijah asked. "Remember when we started this tree house, we were all going to have a job."

"How about if you and Janasa are in charge of painting the walls?" Jeshu suggested.

Elijah and Janasa looked at each other and both shook their heads, agreeing. They would ask Grandpa for any spare paint he might have in his garage. There was bound to be some since Grandpa rarely tossed anything out.

The younger boys, Isaac and Josias, awaited their assignments.

"This place is a mess, full of old leaves and scraps of wood," Janasa said, her hands on her hips as she took a determined look around. "How about if you two start getting rid of it? Just throw it out the windows."

"Oh, boy," Josias said, gathering a handful of leaves and watching as they spilled to the ground. Isaac picked up a stash of wood scraps and pitched them through a window. He looked down as he poked his head from the window, quickly drawing back inside.

"I think I hit a cow," he said.

Sure enough, a cow belonging to Grandpa's next-door neighbor, Farmer Gus, had gotten out and wandered onto the property. Curious, like cows naturally tend to be, she looked up as the kids all tried to cram their heads into the window.

"What in the world is that cow doing?" Beniah asked as she backed into the wooden ladder and started rubbing against it, trying as hard as she could to get rid of an itch.

A rather large cow, she soon toppled the ladder with a crash against another nearby tree, breaking it in two.

"What in the world is that cow doing?"

Frightened, the cow stomped over the broken ladder, further smashing it, before lumbering back to her own field.

"Oh, no," Jeshu exclaimed. "How are we going to get down? Grandma and Grandpa's house is pretty far away, I'm not sure they would hear us if we started yelling."

"Well, if we don't show up for dinner, they might come out looking for us," Beniah said. "But that's a couple of hours away. We're going to be stuck up this tree for a long time."

Janasa reached into the backpack that she, like the other kids, had hauled with her into the tree house. "I brought along a book. I'm perfectly fine to be up here until someone shows up."

"Well, the someone is just going to have to be Grandma and Grandpa," Jeshu said. "Since our parents are off at a business meeting about our moms opening their own bakery. They won't be back until tomorrow."

"I sure wish we had some of their cookies or a cupcake right now," Elijah said sadly.

Isaac reached into his backpack and brought out a candy bar and an orange. Josias dumped out his backpack and found a pack of peanut butter crackers among all the toy cars and trucks.

"Okay," Janasa said, opening her book and preparing to get comfortable on the floor. "At least we won't starve."

A Horn
to the Rescue

An hour passed as Isaac and Josias played with the toy cars and trucks, Janasa read and the older boys played game after game of tic-tac-toe. Waiting to play the winner of the latest game, Elijah's face brightened.

"Why didn't I think of this before?" he shouted, reaching for his unopened backpack. "I have my trumpet in here. I'm supposed to practice this afternoon and totally forgot I had it with me. Maybe I could blow it and get Grandma or Grandpa's attention."

Elijah brought the horn to his mouth and started playing every song he knew.

"No, that's not going to work," Beniah said when neither grandparent showed up. "You need to just blow random notes, something very annoying so it gets their attention. You can't be putting on a nice concert."

Elijah obliged, blowing so many sour notes that everyone covered their ears and screwed up their faces. Finally, Grandpa appeared below.

"What's all that noise?" he yelled up through the branches. "And who smashed up this ladder?"

Talking all at once, they explained what had happened and asked how soon they could be rescued. Grandpa rubbed his beard.

"Umm. Now that could be a problem. That was my only ladder. I don't climb up on roofs anymore, so I sold my other ladders at a yard sale." The kids groaned.

"Now, now, don't get excited. I'll just hop in the truck and go borrow one from the neighbors. You wait here," he said, laughing when he realized they didn't have another choice.

A few minutes later, Grandpa was back, along with Grandma, who had a worried look. "Are you kids all right?" she asked, satisfied when they replied that they were fine, just a little bored was all.

"I have some bad news," Grandpa said. "Old Clunker won't start," he said, referring to his beat-up old truck with the faded red paint and large dent in the fender, not to mention an undependable starter.

"And I can't call anyone because the phone is out. That dang phone has been nothing but trouble ever since we switched companies. It looks like you might be stuck in that  tree house awhile, but you all look pretty comfortable up there. Just think of this as an adventure."

"You always say that Grandpa," Isaac pointed out. "But what about dinner? We ate all our snacks."

"Don't you worry," Grandma said quickly. "I'm going back to the house and I'll make you a meal you'll never forget. I swear, when it comes to you grandkids there's never a dull moment."

11

Send Up
Another Book

"In the meantime, we need to figure out a way to get the food up to you," Grandpa said as he started towards the garage to look for a rope and a bucket. After repeated tries of tossing the rope into the tree, only to have it get tangled in the lower branches, the rope eventually snagged itself on a limb just below the trap door into the tree house. Since he had the longest arms, Jeshu opened the door and reached down, straining to move his fingers just a few inches more towards the rope. He finally grabbed it, pulling it into the room.

"Tie that end onto something so we don't lose the rope and have to try that again," Grandpa shouted.

"Maybe we could tie it around Josias," Elijah suggested.

"No," Beniah said. "That limb right outside the window looks pretty sturdy. We can use that." He double knotted the rope and Jeshu gave it a final tug to make sure it was tight.

"Okay, Grandpa, we're all set," he yelled.

"I'm going to tie the bucket on this end, and we'll use it to carry up your dinner and anything else you might need," Grandpa said.

"I just finished my book," Janasa said. "Could you please send up another one?"

"We need more toy trucks," Josias said, and Isaac asked to have his favorite quilt delivered, the one that had patches of fabric with a cat design.

The bucket went up and down, delivering more blankets and sweatshirts because with Grandpa's phone out and Old Clunker still refusing to start, the kids had no choice but to spend the night confined to the treetops. Grandma returned with a stack of their favorite sandwiches and a container of milk.

"I had cookie dough in the freezer," she said. "So, these are still warm from the oven. And I've sent up some apples."

Everyone settled into the meal, the kids up above and their grandparents sitting in folding chairs below.

"Hey," Grandpa shouted. "Could somebody pass the salt?" The kids just groaned.

Elijah played
"Taps" as the last
bit of sunlight
disappeared.

The sun began to set, and the gang settled in for the night. Luckily, Jeshu and Beniah had built a large enough room that they could all spread out, even though it was rather close.

"We forgot to brush our teeth," Josias yelled to his grandparents.

"You can skip it this time," Grandma called back. "This is sure some situation. It's a good thing our phone is still out, and your parents have no clue about what's going on. But you're safe up there and in the morning, we'll try and get you down if it's the last thing we do. Elijah, blow your trumpet if you need us to come during the night."

They all shouted their good nights and Elijah brought the trumpet to his lips and played "Taps" as the last bit of sunlight disappeared.

Throughout the night Beniah had crazy dreams about being out to sea in a sailing boat and there were squirrels running through the masts.

When Jeshu woke to the loud chirping of birds he immediately yelled to Elijah to stop playing music this early in the morning. Isaac wrapped his quilt tighter and said he was fed up with all the adventure.

Janasa happily discovered that Fred, Grandpa's cat, had climbed up into the tree house during the night. She gathered him into her arms and listened to him purring.

"I sure wish we had claws like a cat," Elijah said. "Then we could get down if we wanted to."

"Actually, I'm enjoying being up here," Janasa said. "Except for being crammed together with all you stinky boys and your smelly socks. I'm thinking this will make a good story for the school newspaper when school starts in the fall. I'll bet it will be on the front page."

"Good morning, kids," Grandpa's voice boomed from below. "Sounds like everyone made it through the night."

Hatching a Plan

——————

"**D**o you have a game plan for getting us down?" Jeshu asked, leaning out the window while Josias and Isaac clamored about having a plan for getting their breakfast sent up.

Janasa worried about wearing the same clothes two days in a row. Meanwhile, Beniah and Elijah were trying to figure out a way down using the rope coiled at their feet.

"One thing at a time," Grandpa said. "First things first. I finally got a signal on my phone and called the fire department to bring over a ladder."

Josias and Isaac jumped up and down and squealed with excitement at having a fire truck show up.

"Thing is," Grandpa said, "they only have the one truck, and they need it on a barn fire way out in the country, further out than we are. I called Farmer Gus and he's in the middle of delivering a calf, but he does have a ladder."

Grandpa cleared his throat. "Except that Old Clunker still isn't starting and we can't haul a ladder with Grandma's car. Bottom line, you'll have to stay where you are for a little longer."

With an armful of food, Grandma showed up at the bottom of the tree. "Who wants pancakes? Send down the bucket so I can get these delivered while they're still warm."

With breakfast finished, Jeshu and Beniah invented a game to pass the time, tossing down walnuts as Grandpa ran back and forth with a baseball mitt trying to catch them. Every time he missed, Grandpa had to run around the tree backwards, or hop around on one leg while singing "Take Me Out to the Ball Game."

"Okay, enough of trying to kill Grandpa," he said breathlessly, sinking into a lawn chair. "I think it's time for you to come up with a way of entertaining yourselves. I'm going inside and get my phone so I can see what's keeping the fire company and whether Farmer Gus has finished delivering that calf. We need to get this show on the road."

But there was no news for most of the day, especially after Grandpa's cell phone again went on the fritz.

After lunch, all six kids, one by one, fell asleep, full of Grandma's sloppy Joes. Fred liked being in the tree house with all them, curling up in the space between Isaac and Josias.

Before drifting off, Beniah wondered if they couldn't use Isaac's blanket as a parachute and Jeshu thought dragging a trampoline to the bottom of the tree would create a soft landing if they jumped.

"I think I'm done having this adventure," Elijah said, closing his eyes. "It was fun at first, but not so much anymore."

In the middle of their naps, the kids were awakened by the noise of Grandpa and Farmer Gus carrying a ladder between them. "Here we go, it's the rescue crew," Grandpa shouted as they set the ladder against the tree, only to find that it was too short.

"Dang," said Farmer Gus, "I thought for sure this would work. But we have another plan. Don't you kids worry. And I'm as sorry as can be that my cow smashed up your ladder. If it hadn't been for her none of this would have happened."

Grandpa and Gus walked in the direction of Gus's barn and the kids wondered what they had planned.

"Maybe there really will be a trampoline, just like I said before," Jeshu suggested.

"I think maybe Farmer Gus has some kind of big bird that can swoop in here and carry us to the ground," said Josias. "I just hope the claws won't hurt too much."

"Yeah, right," Janasa said, rolling her eyes. "I bet they're just going for a longer ladder."

"Maybe it will be a machine that Farmer Gus uses to get up in the trees to pick apples," Beniah said. "That would be so much fun to ride down on that thing."

"I think you're all wrong," said Elijah. "I think the fire department is finally going to show up and rescue us."

"But how will the fire truck get back here through all the other trees?" asked Isaac. "There's no road. They can't drive a big fire truck back here."

"Hey, here they come," Jeshu said, leaning out the window. "It looks like they're riding on a hay wagon and it's being pulled by a horse." The kids jumped up and down with excitement, scaring the squirrel family in the tree's upper branches.

Grandpa and Gus pulled the wagon with its big load of fluffy hay beneath the tree. "Okay, who wants to go first?" Grandpa called up.

"You mean you want us to jump into that pile of hay?" Jeshu asked.

"That's the idea," said Farmer Gus. "It's piled up good and high and it will be like landing on your bed at home."

"Oh, boy!" said Isaac who regularly gets into trouble for jumping on his bed. The others were just as excited and they decided that Josias, being the youngest, would go first. The other kids would be behind him to give him encouragement.

Jeshu picked up his brother and eased him through the trap door, holding him under his arms. "Ready?" Josias squeezed his eyes shut and with a quiver in his voice said he was. Jeshu let go and Josias landed right on top of the hay pile, sinking down so that Grandpa had to pull him out.

"That was fun!" Josias shouted, brushing hay off his clothes. "You should all try it."

Isaac went next, sending out a whoop when he landed.

Janasa followed, making sure she remembered every bit of the experience for the story she was planning to write for the school newspaper.

Elijah blasted his trumpet right before taking his leap and Beniah and Jeshu decided to grab the rope, swing, and then jump from it when they were over the hay wagon.

"Everyone okay?" Grandpa asked, looking them over. "And by the way, welcome back to Earth."

The kids ran to the house to tell Grandma that they had been rescued, although she heard the commotion long before they burst through the door.

"It's a good thing Grandpa and Gus got you down from there, your parents will be here in time for dinner and I sure wouldn't want to tell them you were stuck in a tree," she said.

Later that night, after taking baths and finally getting to brush their teeth, the kids asked if they could all sleep in the living room since they were used to being together all those hours. They spread out their blankets and fluffed up the pillows. Isaac picked a few stray pieces of hay from his quilt and Fred the cat found an empty spot next to Josias where he could curl up.

"First thing tomorrow we're going to need to find a replacement ladder," Jeshu said.

"And this time we'll make sure it stays where it's supposed to," Beniah said.

"I think I want to wait a bit before I go back up there," Janasa said, "Although it was sure a great adventure. How about you, Elijah?"

Elijah was getting groggy, but managed to mumble just before falling asleep, "I think I'm going to miss living with all those squirrels."

THE END

About the Author

NANCY LUSE has had a lengthy career as a newspaper reporter and editor and is currently assistant editor at *Frederick Magazine*, Frederick, Md., where she resides. Additionally, she has written for regional and national publications and has been honored with numerous awards for her work.

She is the author of *More than the Meal*, a collection of food columns gathered into a book from her years at *The Frederick News-Post* where she also wrote a blog, *Another One Rides the Bus*, about her daily experiences commuting by city transit. A two-act comedy, *Bus Buddies*, soon followed and was staged multiple times for Frederick audiences.

At Home Among the Squirrels is Nancy's first published children's book, joining a children's holiday serial, *The J-Boys and the Miracle Mail*, which appeared in *The News-Post*.

About the Artist

GILLIAN GROZIER was trained at the Arts Students League in New York City and later studied painting in Katonah, N.Y., where she was a member of the Westchester Art Society and Mamaroneck Artists' Guild. She won the Audubon Artists Michael M. Engels, Sr. Award and taught painting under the Chappaqua, N.Y. Adult Education Program.

Gillian followed a professional career as a writer and a poet, becoming a founding member of Lingua, a published poets' workshop. Under the Lingua aegis, she created an illustrated epic titled Enki's Flood, based on Sumerian mythology before returning full time to the visual arts in 2010. Since that time, as a regular exhibitor in New York and Connecticut galleries and museums, she won awards in 2014 and 2015 for her watercolors from the Darien Arts Center in Fairfield County, Conn. She moved to Frederick, Md., in 2016.

CPSIA information can be obtained
at www.ICGtesting.com
Printed in the USA
BVHW091101230621
610212BV00010B/1735